Orchids

JT WELSCH grew up in Waterloo, Illinois, a small farm town across the Mississippi River from St. Louis. Earlier this year, he completed a PhD in Manchester, where he currently lives, writes, and teaches at various universities. *Orchids* is his first book of poetry.

Orchids

by

JT WELSCH

SALT

LONDON

PUBLISHED BY SALT PUBLISHING
Dutch House, 307–308 High Holborn, London WC1V 7LL United Kingdom

© JT Welsch, 2010

The right of JT Welsch to be identified as the
author of this work has been asserted by him in accordance
with Section 77 of the Copyright, Designs and Patents Act 1988.

Salt Publishing 2010

Printed and bound in the United Kingdom by Lightning Source UK Ltd

Typeset in Swift 9.5 / 13

ISBN 978 1 84471 802 3 paperback

1 3 5 7 9 8 6 4 2

Contents

Acknowledgements

Much credit and gratitude is due to the editors of the following publications, where versions of some of these poems have appeared: *Bewilderbliss, Blackbox Manifold, Boston Review, The Manchester Review*, and *The Red Wheelbarrow*.

Orchids

Because there are orchids
looking after man's already
fragile systems, our queer hero
hangs over a bridge, his V.O.
muddled by the foley work
on a half-thawed river sizing
up his wobbly station wagon:

"Dearest, the only type of
drowning I dread transpires
in the stifling privacy of a shed
of one's own, with one's shield
or upon it. But how to put it,
and where? How to abdicate,
to bravely puppeteer one

split-moment into the drink
—stealing past the idle air,
icy air, ice crust surplus and...
spl-gulp before the *shhh*. Best case,
accomplished, if I do say so,
and I do, it seems, at the cost
of any realistic security, ever."

The Mirror Stage

There I am, Lord Leighton's
Flaming June, blu-tacked
at the foot of the bed, a trick
of perspective in the fuzzy,

Pre-Raphaelite light of dawn.
Back from where our toes meet,
urged by the kiss in every crease
of that eponymous silk flame,

I expand into thighs drawn up
toward such a torso. More than
the obvious spill of hair, I feel
sea air moving over my arms

and my jaw from a window
not behind my dreaming head.
Nothing completely breaks the
spell. I choose to remain hopeful.

Dún Laoghaire Postcard

You'd think I already had myself homesick for
homesickness, but don't forget my hatred of the sea,
the unsteadiness I claim within a hundred miles.

Basically, England? A painting in the corridor
is one my mom's parents had. After breakfast,
I lay back down at a window facing the famous pier.

Waiting for my epiphany, I daydreamed of Papa
tossing that gift-shop sand-dollar a few yards ahead
of Grammy, who'd been hunting one all afternoon.

Do me a favour: Look up why the ocean fizzles
where it touches land. Is it that air gets in (or out)
at the creases? I'm making *thought* water, *being* earth,

and *language* the waves between, which reminds me,
a souvenir's en route. No offense, but you don't seem
to own a lot of my most loved of your belongings.

[3]

Meditation on Washing Up

I

I feel no duty toward these dishes, even if
I'll be the last to read them, or their splotches,
and quickly, till each re-surfaces,
more complete than I ever hope to be.

II

It's not like what we do with a gentler sponge,
uprooting whatever's been determined
(in this circular way) to be outside us.
Nothing outside us makes us dirty, says Jesus.

III

Who'd believe it's invisibly small creatures
eating and shitting dead skin that does it?
Uncleanliness is a feature of neither dirt nor thing,
but teeters between, like any other fornication.

IV

Absolution is an endless archaeology.
Every plate you bring into our home is held
to its inscription, waiting, or jumping the queue
to don the colours that say *Mine* or *Hers*.

I know I'm clearing what can't add to our re-births.
That's why I like washing you even more
than dishes: insane jealousy of your microbes.
Unlike food's, I savour their downfall. Plus...

If my own troops have more spunk, so to speak,
they're only half me, and equally erasable.
Mark 7:19—What goes down identifies
temporarily with body, not the soul.

A Rejection of Marriage

The earliest memory you're ready to share
is pretending to sleep in the pram.
The moral in this is obscure,
though I'm sure it has one,
as surely as the rejection of marriage
by all those doctors in your French novels,
each called to some higher calling or other.

Only *The Wood Demon* comes
to my poorly-read mind. As surely as it
leads to marriage, I was going to say.
It isn't true. What actually happens
is just what you'd expect. Don't laugh!
Even if you suffered Earth alone
for four months, pre-widowed infant,

twenty-seven years estranged, we both
happened to be five once, little bunny.
You had a fat face and an already
haunting stare for the disaster at the far end
of your mother's camera. I recall none
of your other early habits now,
but I should learn to trust my notes.

La Grande Guerre Façades (1964)

René Magritte

She postures at the floodwall,
sea flush with sky, parasol
balanced on right shoulder
behind a hat as wide and
as laden with feathers
to match the clouds, like all
but the leaves of the posy
of lilacs suspended at her face.
Her frock buttons at the neck.
Edwardian dress, I see now,
making certain it's his mother.
In the dark, through river trees,
he chases his kid brother, who
helps drag out what he's spotted
in the moonlight. They unwrap
the dressing gown gathered
at its face, as again, my hands
fall silent on you in the dark.

The Man from the Phone Company

A man from the phone company
hoists his great blue handset,
settling on the savage rhythms
it will accentuate for him.

I watch because I cannot listen.
In town, you're buying something
you found last week, not hidden
in the library, as I've told him.

While he works, I see your paper-
white, down-penciled belly until
another stone-eyed blackbird
has a go at our leafless grapes,

nearly as dark as it by now.
The man has taken no notice.
My heart goes out to hands like
his, like paws. I need their pity.

Baseball

Forget PVC. Double-knit polyester,
you'll find, can be worn as snugly.
It also shows the straps of subtle codpieces
looping the thighs and buttocks
giving these new boys such power.

Leave the stilettos and whips at home.
They've got nothing on metal-studded cleats,
or leather gloves wringing a greased-up
club as he lowers into then bobs a little
in a stance, adjusting, holding 80,000

eyeballs in the *sang-froid* of his glare.
It's this authority, such wildness reined
into the forgone instant of his wallop,
driving the long, slow-motion arc
of our release. High fives all around.

A Late Cary Grant as Sherlock Holmes

Randy Scott will play Doc Watson,
to whom I'll never actually say
"Elementary, my dear..."
He's so much more convincing
as an Englishman. Chaplin dodged
that bullet. I sound like T.S. Eliot.

"Oh, where in the crowd of our
old Irregulars, in the clouds of perfume
with all shutters drawn,
do these damned things go missing?"
My mother's been the only
real mystery, living or undead.

No one would dare say publicly,
of course, but the only difference
between Jim and Monty,
between your dorm room wall
and the longest, loveliest suicide in Hollywood
is a couple of lousy miles an hour.

Believe me, I've earned the drugs.
For once, I want the world
to see me in disguise. Everyone wants
to be me, but *ratiocination* means
I'm in every noggin but my own.
"What's the O stand for?"

Nothing. Oh, oh, oh...
That's exactly what it stands for.
To be cruel, I've had to learn to be emotional.
Something of the body must
outlive the violence. Remind me
to tell you about my year in St. Louis.

Screen Tests

JAMES DEAN READING FOR SAL MINEO

Don't worry, you said. Nobody stays dead,
except Bucky, Jason Todd, and Uncle Ben.
It was true then, that summer Superman came back
simultaneously as a black guy, some kid,
a cyborg, and a meaner alien.
Besides, I trusted you, to the point
where I now come off like the Grand Inquisitor:
Is it thou, you son of a bitch? You'll ruin everything.
In fact, your faith in me has always been in vain.

SAL MINEO READING FOR JAMES DEAN

Tonight, sweet Lyosha, in the wretched gap
when the far edge of Tuesday's daylight
passes the grille of your screen door,
but the next has yet to swing back round mine,
as our hemisphere constricts,
I'd love to find a roost within your fiery breast.
If only one of us had a pen, or a knife, or a penknife,
to marry us with one gash, a vinculum,
since "what's essential is invisible to the eyes..."

The Artist as the Head of Goliath (c. 1610)

Caravaggio

I

I knew his grip in my hair,
darling twigger, the mute
bellying blood velvet, then
foisted like a lamp to gander
into this long room, dying
to spot that other Michelangelo.

II

Still awaiting what signal.
Our stage beyond that curtain
turned out to be an airport
Hilton shower, and I'm alone.
Where fly you, dear Perseus,
my stripling Jew? Fly home.

III

Swooning again the steam,
having absently sliced a nipple
on an ill-willed jag of tiny soap,
bullied little linga, my child,
like the figurehead of the Argo,
finds its voice and kills a joke.

Rievaulx Abbey

We are transcended in some shots
facing back over the ruins
of Helmsley Castle, before
retreating for Cornish ice cream:

sheep like a field of stars below.
They were here, long enough
to build it is what matters.
French, that's your domain,

but the Church too, I suppose.
Too busy with the camera to consider it.
Consider what didn't occur to you!
Howling stairwells to nowhere,

larking in archways upholding
nothing. God? Ineffable faces,
the pageboy bob, no trace,
although you swear you knew.

"All women know." Did I take
comfort in that? The reveal ever
at the horizon, and Castle Howard!
Why didn't you say it was so near?

Maybe tainted, maybe haunted
or brought to a kind of ruin
by such scenes, but surely no
betrayal of your National Trust.

The Virgin in Prayer

In Waterstone's across from Victoria
with a few fussy minutes to spare, I picked up
a new book of translations by Tom Paulin,
which, with a shudder undiminished by years,
I remember closing loudly at the rendering
of Heine as *making a meal of your cunt.*

The weekend itself is lost entirely.
Thank God she lied about her period,
having vowed not to get involved too quickly.
The year before, evangelicals were the answer,
that is, until one of their stepfathers' hands
fell on my shoulder during grace.

The Pelagian Heresy

Now is the time for all good men to come to the aid of their party.

Does this goodness hinge
on what aid one has time for,
or more the party's needs?
In which case, the baptism

was a fucking ruse. We know
something dramatic has occurred.
The age-old question of intent
remains. Drunk or no, my twin

will have her scars. Yes, Br. Alex,
vertical. Qu'importe? Maybe you're
tempted to see a curse, maybe
something of our blood set loose.

Twins. Maybe tempted to dial up
that myth? Point of fact, of her,
I feel little but an urge to confess
the urge to confess the urge

to confess, ad hominem, etc.
Oh, and guilt. What stops here if
I've speeded, endangering party
lives, or if I shaved my legs one

January afternoon and found them
identical to hers, or failed to say
I'm also an electrician because
it made his descriptions of things

I'd agreed to hand up if he let me
watch sound so elegant? Never
will I marry so long as my heart's face
faces the sun and hates the darkness.

Coppice

Yes, it's cutbacks time. This winter,
the planet is in brilliant recession.
Contemptible new lines of sight are
daily being opened up and up and up
for sinners in the hands of an angry Dow.

No one's buying any solution back home.
No one will see the copse for the corpses.
When they cleared along the mill path,
my own gut-of-guts' reaction was that
we shouldn't see our house from here.

The sign calls coppicing an ancient art,
but that doesn't make it common sense.
Cutting back to help grow? Admit it,
invisible hand: Diversity's a hard sell.
If nothing else, who's your target audience?

If it were natural, the argument goes,
Miss Nature would regulate herself.
But nature isn't rational, not like a soul!
So, we'll wager the organic, working body
against an otherwise uninsured salvation:

A penny saved *qua* a penny earned.
Substitute your paper currency of choice.
You don't understand: It's in my blood.
My forefathers and foremothers robbed
Indian graves to get through their winter.

So what if the Mayflower is a barn in
"Buckinghamshire"? Recycling's cheap.
Cut the canopy, let the underwood breathe.
God can whip up a zillion new trees.
I'll bet none of them come with poems.

Formby

Individual mudflats and sandflats, embryonic
shifting dunes. Fixed and mobile dunes
of the mobile dune system, with humid dune slacks
and dune grasslands. Dune heat among the reedbeds
and various other bedforms at Formby, ringed
with ringed plover, grey plover, grey-haired
grey hair grass and bar-tailed godwit. Knot, dunlin,
and stable bar features on the foreshore, near the windfarm.
Liverwort, penny and sneeze wort, sea sandwort.
Sand sedge, sea spurge, wood sage, sand couch, sea kale,
sea rocket, sand lizard, sandwinning, sanderling.
Sea holly and see sandhill rustic moth, and most mosses,
saltmarsh, polypody, kidney vetch, then restharrow.
Do dewberry. Wintering waterfowl or individual
waders on the strandline. Helleborine. Cowline thistle,
horsetail, cat's tails or cat's ears, mouse-eared hawkweed,
hawksbeard, colt's foot, bird's foot trefoil, viper's bugloss,
false catgrass, true bee orchid, marsh orchid, or $10,000
pyramidal orchid. Catch the oystercatcher and scattered
bricks, or broken brick chimneys (for sea defences),
and famed natterjack toads, known locally as the
Bootle Organ. Dogs, still and silent in their station
wagon pens. The world's first world's first lifeboat station.
Two dads with two girls. Two mums with two girls'
four wellies. The fantastic great-crested newt, yellow-
horned poppy, or too few few-flowered spike-rush.
Shy red squirrels, acquiescing to American grays.
The red deer's 5000-year-old footprints on or in
the beach, with those of the auroch, the last of which
died in Poland, 1627, before the initial resilience
of the Saxons when the Vikings rowed from Ireland,

before the last launch from the lifeboat station was filmed,
1916, before the Romans, before the railway bringing
human manure from Liverpool, before Liverpool,
well before your uncle, the chemist, was born
and eventually reborn Father Formby.

Resurrection Man

We "abused" the all-day passes? What was Edinburgh denied,
hopping on and off only to dig through secondhand books?

That was my mother's word for it on the drive back south,
bringing my anti-tourism into her broader critique of our

then "not typical" arrangement, twisting around up front
with the reading lamp still strapped to her aging forehead.

At least we heard four or five equally fantastic body counts
for Burke and Hare, each time we passed the med school.

Does it matter which one of their hands became a wallet?
She doesn't buy Deconstructionism. The more the merrier,

I say. Two heads and all that. In the end, the Rock held out,
and Parliament was the ugly stitch-up that is democracy.

"We'll always have parataxis," I sigh, throwing the switch.
No joy. Eventually, we all go green, though I do wonder

how she's getting on. Don't I? Hadn't thought of it till now,
seeing you off to honest work. I know I'm the resurrection.

He Do *Star Wars* In Different Voices

The facts. No dirty talk. No reference,
no puns. Would it be easier
just to watch the damn things?
Maybe, sweetheart, it would've been.
We'll agree it's too late now.

To spare my nostalgia for some
pure edition no one has ever seen,
I shield you, in turn, with these hours
and awful English accents, a bed sheet
for an all-purpose prop and costume.

For you, we take as much time
doubling back for Kurosawa,
or Joseph Campbell, for Ben Burtt fun-facts
and the truth about Han and Leia's kids
as we spend lost in headlong exposition.

If that sounds oppressive, I can't help it.
I'm ready to fall on my light saber
belaboring the elegant structures
of the *Expanded Universe*,
expanding on it until it includes you too.

Bed

Why do you say you won't fly with me
to America? No, I don't have to ask.
You've lain in the bed there where we
have lain, you and I, but also she and I.
You don't have to ask. You won't fly.
You "don't want to die." But you will!

"Not just yet," you mean. August, then?
I'm not sure that works as an excuse.
We have our own bed now, a great
white iron frame thing you pore over
like a loony every time I accidentally
ding my belt on it, getting undressed.

There's that tiny divot in the plaster
on the ceiling already, where I hit it,
hurrying to put everything together
our first morning here while you slept
on the floor in what is now your office.
I look for it first thing every morning.

The Vine

One thought is the white vine
in the shed, by which we're both
quite spooked. The bramble
that appeared out front last week
took our heaviest knife,

but still posed less a threat
than this anemic freak, maybe
since she hadn't said a thing
before it had turned the corner behind
the luggage and started up the wall.

The metaphor was too obvious, initially.
Vines? I turned to Dionysus'
double-birth, hoping that might tie it
to Caravaggio's early portrait
where he comes across so sickly himself.

But there was nothing in the reference
to relieve the sense of inevitability
as it goes on climbing in the dark,
against all decency, nothing
to ally us again on any terms but fear.

Echo

As often as the miserable cry'd,
'Alas!' 'Alas,' the wofull Nymph reply'd.
— OVID

Before graduating and heading out east,
my twelve-year-old self lay with chicken-
bone arms folded across his naked chest,
listening with awful grown-up patience

to the house in all its country darkness.
These were the only shameful moments.
When his older sisters', baby brother's,
and at last his parents' rooms fell silent

down the hallway, he could sail to the door,
pulling up the handle to close it halfway,
to listen out. Then the closet light came on,
only enough to catch the bashful outline

in the mirror trying different things from
a trunk downstairs. I remember the chains
on the others' ceiling fans plinking against
their fixtures, and freezing whenever the

rhythm changed. Daytime would've been
smarter, but less romantic. That poor kid's
hair was skater-length soon, and he'd hold it
above his head, letting a glamorous, dark

strand fall over his ears and, later, the curve
of his jaw. He scribbled exact plans for when
he'd live alone and far away, as I do now.
One plain red gown's string that tied above

the waist is here, where only I would notice.
It's enough. If the loss get less imaginary
by the year, in even the most stifled echo,
the more convincing part still finds release.

Marriage

If I ever think of pedaling alongside
the Charles some foggy morning, five years
before our first meeting, I can't help picturing
you then in Oxford or in Nantes: You scan
the Loire with your heavy backpack, then new.
I'll pretend you're on your way to see
the American friends whose peanut butter
I've since vouched for. Tell me, what else
should I be able to deduce these days from
the too-careful click of your office door?

In another hour, I'll watch you undress
against the curtain glowing from the street.
And far too late tomorrow morning,
our bony bodies will lie fastened by each other
along their length, dreaming ourselves down,
following your anxious glance beneath
the surface of that river. A good little historian,
you'd have been pondering "republican marriages",
where priests and nuns were supposedly
stripped, bound back to back, and drowned.

On one hand, my faith in you probably
relates to the exactness of your naked edges,
but like most else now, it ultimately depends
upon your less straightforward presence
among all known pasts and futures
as together, we descend centuries of night
to where others appear, not tragically—
ropes long rotted, but hands still clasped
since their exposure to a far-fetched world,
in that way answering their own prayer for us.

Heimath (Home)

Friedrich Hölderlin

In secret, I pluck
the berries along these
trails, quenching
my lust for the world,

which opens at mid-day
to rose thorns and
the scent of basswood
mixed with beech.

My ear strains toward
the fallow cornfield
for first whispers of the
push toward autumn.

I think of the oaks
forming a kind of nave
while distant chimes
ring, so familiar,

the hour when birds
are due to awaken
and everything will
be as it should be.

Camille sur son lit de mort (1879)

Claude Monet

O, green wife,
diffused, meter

from medium,
you-of-myself,

relic of a will's
last drop mis-

spoken by this
depthless air

into the latest
synthetic oils,

an orifice of it
traced in these

unsound terms
of landscape—

Lightning Source UK Ltd.
Milton Keynes UK
UKOW050607231012

201018UK00002B/3/P